Earthwork

Philip Radmall
Earthwork

Acknowledgements

Poems in this collection have appeared in
Stand Magazine (UK), *Grandchildren of Albion* (UK), *Overland*,
Live Wires, *Light on Don Bank*, *Coastline* (Newcastle Poetry Prize
Anthology 2012), *Now You Shall Know* (Newcastle Poetry Prize
Anthology 2013), *Once Wild* (Newcastle Poetry Prize Anthology
2014), *Can I Tell You a Secret?*

'Grounding' was awarded third prize in the
Newcastle Poetry Prize 2012.

'Festival' was commended in the Newcastle Poetry Prize 2013.

'The Difference of Distance' was awarded third prize in the
Newcastle Poetry Prize 2014.

Earthwork
ISBN 978 1 74027 399 6
Copyright © text Philip Radmall 2017
Cover image: *Sower with Setting Sun*, Vincent van Gogh

First published 2017 by
GINNINDERRA PRESS
PO Box 3461 Port Adelaide 5015 Australia
www.ginninderrapress.com.au

Contents

Greening	7
Seascape	8
Rock of Ages	10
Grounding	11
Matins	16
Remember *The Ducie*?	18
Penelope on the Beach	19
Eden Farm	21
The Difference of Distance	23
Stone Gatherer	30
The Skaters	31
The Hover Fly	32
Thames Ditton Churchyard Revisited	33
Leyton	35
Hart Field	37
Scrumping	38
The Bottom Fields	39
Women Digging Potatoes	41
Couch Adrift	42
A Prospect of the Sea	43
Times Like These	45
Transitions	48
A Wiltshire Church Open Day	49
Losings	51
Festival	53
The Chickens at Summer Keep	61
Kangaroo	62
Pigeons	63
Horror scope	64
The Inlet	65

Wood Gathering	67
Hawks Nest	69
Memory	71
Stone Country	72
The Well	81
Many a True Word…	84
Early Morning, Ramsgate Harbour	86
Canterbury Cathedral	87
At Empress Falls	89

Greening

How seamlessly you move through the garden
and the still morning air, letting the butcher bird's
a cappella stay and resonate with you,
there amongst the weft of sight and sound,
bound to your essential world. Your bare arms
cool the light as your hands stroke out
the season's new buds into the day, tend
to old stems, settle and ease the moist, dark soils.
Leaves lie pooled in rain; shadows anchor
to tree bark against the sun's drifting stealth.
Come inside now and breakfast
on fruits and grains and creams
where my own heart's rhythm calls;
bring me your calm and the freshness
of grevillea, orchid, maiden hair, the sense
of this place where I too can be and grow.

Seascape

Once you have come this far, for however long,
by whatever path, stand out on the edge
of the dunes, just enough away from the sea,
the white sand rippled then stretched wet between,
and listen to your heart, in a quiet halt of time;
catch its intimate, meticulous age,
the way the slow surf pulls and ruffles up
over the drag of a rock; or how the waters of the ledge pools
stay off the tide, the recurrence of flood,
and wait and show themselves stilled and suspended
in a glassed capture of light and reflection and calm.
Let the heart's beat steady you to this ground.
Too many times it runs on distracted, or rattles loose,
churns and falters, forced to gather in
hard deposits from all else around;
let it ease, like the low sun soothes the air
softening the earth's topography, the farnesses
beyond; settle now the old geology of the blood.
I think we should always take a moment to be
where we are, and know ourselves there;
like you went up to that man, any man,
just to talk, to feel part of things again,
because there is always so much wrong otherwise,
the years peeling themselves away; how they have
the look often of that paperbark tree in your garden,
but which still stands firm, anchored, historied,
unashamed by the loss of itself.

So wait, before the instinct moves you on again:
a long flocked line of cormorants passing
suddenly overhead, locked in staggered formation
heading to the distance, taking the heart with them.

Rock of Ages

What I see in this cold, smooth scallop of brown rock
shucked from the dank waterhole and held out
to fit your cupped palm, is the blank face of a god
we don't believe in, showing us humble through
a hint of what lies sure, powerful, resolute beyond us.

After our descent into the base of this tall,
thick overgrowth, we stand finally in the denser shades
within the cool, still catchment, as if low in the earth,
my feet unsure against the uneven give of the bank,
amongst the ferns and vines edging its slope;
yours in further across the stones, encroached
over the shallow water, your body calm, diligent,
come up against this piece of old inertia
that you hold up through its millions of years,
anchoring us to its mute discovery.

Your face burns alive, gleeful, distracted, fathoming
the rock's weight, its surface; like we should take it,
harbour it in the globed corner of a small room,
attend to it amongst us: own it and consider;
archetype of resilience and temperance and change.
We look down together into the clear, flat bed
of the water teeming with grit and pebbles,
a small, patient congregation of other rocks,
then back at your find. Before we move on
into another part of our limited day,
you yield it back, out of your open hand,
slow, respectful, stooping to avoid a splash.

Grounding

1 Farringdon

All was whiteness as I walked my way,
heavily shod and gloved and garmented,
half tenderly across the open fields of snow
rising broad and clear towards Farringdon;
the surface yielding only to compact.
This was winter's tundra: bleached anathema
to the warmth of blood and life; things
staunched and numbed in smothered ground.
Onwards, more steadily, I trudged the ruts
of an old track marking a faint route still
to a high ridge and frosted copse.
Underfoot raised ribbed earth, glazed in ice,
awkward to tread; veined leaves cast
frail into the withered mud; the land's
chilled flesh thin and brittle to the touch.

Easy here to fail and fear the world's
lean and frozen body inert beneath
the steely air. I must grip every
footfall down else lose hold of things;
look hard through the blanched calm
and brave this season, cold as bone;
return some time to see these fields green again
and feel the warm ground's soft, familiar skin.

2 Bedrock

Remember that walk along the undercliff,
the track cut in against the massive edge
of the escarpment, when we stopped to feel
the immaculate bank of strata, levelled
and angled into the overhang;
to touch the whole complex geology,
the movement and anchoring of ground,
its long interminable settlement
through fathomless time. In your room I watch
your upright, easeful, solitary drift
towards the bed, wonder at the fact of you
sliding between the sheets' surfaces next to me.
We too bear outward signs: tentative
but forceful workings of our history
come physical; adumbrations fixed
in the seeming stillness of the body.
Like I might read each meaning to your life
set down in your shape and form,
annotated in the skin and become
accessible. Like when you traced the clear
intricate layers of sedimented stone.

It is what I notice as you tell me things:
the goosebumps risen along your thigh; the marks
from your womb; the thin, faint lines of vein;
a fleck of damaged flesh: years of discovery
and loss; the long pull of motherhood;
a reaching for some old paternal hold;
the close, coarse contact of others drawn
against the ageing grain of your side.
Like this is a way to connect; the slow
momentous changes gleaned from what still lies
exposed. Our lives are implicated
in the accumulations of the past.
Yet what we are and love and understand
is now and here; our ground come together;
our histories only bearing us as the next
deposits of our age are laid down,
settle, and build, like these sheets,
over our bedrock, our shallow depth of time.

3 Cunjurong Point

Beyond the high dunes, the beach, the terminus
of tide and shore, the sea pulls back, uncovering
the raw mass of the rock ledge rising out
of the sand flats, a stark, black plateau
undercut and dissected, depth and surface
open into the sun. It is as if the world
wants us to see the difficult handiwork
of its age, the basalt and quartz and grain
of its old material unearthed under the tight
pull of the stretched ocean. And if we move
onto this painful ground we come across
findings more immense, epitomised
and particular; marks when things changed
or died; the extinctions of species leaving
their ghosts in the rock; remnants of their passing
embedded in the contiguous whole
which leads to us here, alive and now.

Come out across my own ledge of rough time
towards where I too am marked by an end;
walk the brief jagged edge that leads to it, bouldered
and sharded, part of my quickened age,
till you sight the faint, intricate imprint left there.
Touch it as you touch me; it is that thin
shiver that runs through; the stark, inanimate look
bearing loss and aftermath; a semblance of a life
perished and fossilised into my rock.
And beside it the struggle of what lies
loose still in the pooled hollows of its baulk,
churned by the continuing wash of the sea.

Return then to the beach to go on further
knowing what you know; forgive the awkward
ground which forms me, as the sea recovers
and draws in. Tread back along
the softer edge of the articulate surf
at the reach and limits of the tide
where sea and rock are reconciled
and the ground appeases, smooth again to the foot.

Matins

for Carol

I am with the still now of the lake at morning,
quiet as in a vestibule. Before me, in the fuss
of its years, the ancient, venerable hill

puts on its glimmering vestments, holds itself
to the light and smoothens the heavy folds
of shadow that tumble down its hump and form

into the grace of the lake's low lie; out to the middle
where a few sparse congregations of trees
stand islanded and bowed to the water surface

that flows past and through like a strong faith.
But everywhere I look now into this landscape there is
the pull of light and shade across it, reminding me

that all is never quite certain, never quite settled;
a mattering about it like the mark of a frown
on the face of an old god troubled by his works.

As we prepare for another day here together,
I look at you curled on the bed, in the crimps of dawn,
concede again to a check of conscience as I think

how others had to die to bring us here, their loss
become our find; an unlikely irony
cast across our forming, making us too seem

deepened by things, suffused, interspersed:
always something furrowed upon our ground.
But hard to see us different, or more humble

when we see each day as incremental still, remaining,
the great draw of their come and go; it is as if
I am a man hammering iron, watching the sparks

arcing to the floor, cooling, darkening to sweepings,
as you come sloshing water from a pale,
losing some of the fresh-fetched hold in glinting spills

dashed and drowned across the shimmering grass:
always seeing one thing set against another.
Though never shall I want us otherwise than we are.

As you stir, the green, garmented hill holds itself
to the light again, as if in discipline to its office
and its labour, bearing its rumpled shadows.

So our fate stands better gathered over, like
pleated folds hung down some dread and dutiful cloth
shaping out the dazzle of a robe.

Remember *The Ducie*?

Sometimes in my garden's backdrop of bush
there's the sudden rummage of a leaf dropping
sounding as if it is trying to question
why things are. Like my older voice now
sounding back to the place which first
held me sure, through many other leaf-falls
of times and meanings, all that's done and not done.

It was long ago when we first met,
sitting around a table in an old pub
full of gaunt men and fiddles,
dark pints and stuttering tunes;
games of darts in the small back parlour.
But we were aimed differently and never stuck.
Yet I can still recall and understand
all that was said then and done.
There are years of distance between there and here,
but if every day were the same thought
what passes is just the interstices between
and the meaning stays with us as it was.
It is only the past ageing, not us.
We stay within the slow echo
of events dropping away, the dim
resonance of falling things,
darts on a beer soaked floor.

Now as you go into a new decade
feel the echoes, the landings
of memory, the ground that succours
and still succours when the leaves fall.

Penelope on the Beach

Are there no other good men out there, I ask,
enough to free the cage-rattling heart,
relieve the burdened years of memories,
or check the onslaught of life's harsh pattern;
only pale-livered warriors who will yield
like me to the slow encroachment
of the final absence of air and thought and love.
Otherwise, who finds me here helps me
with nothing of what was or what will come,
alone in this careering, unsynchronised time.
Those who wait are the first to feel
and the last to know; weaving love out of patience,
unravelling faith from faithlessness.
Even the weeds lost and stranded at my heels
obey the quiet oracle of the sea
succumbing to the tumbling waves
which, as I walk, bountifully bathe my feet
whilst erasing my soft, shallow footfalls.

Further out I see the clear sky shimmer
upon the thick meniscus of the water,
the sea's deep constancy betrayed
by the complexity of its surface,
and all my own confusions mingled there.
But before the good god calls
summoning the last tide, and the waves
retreat forever from off this shallow shore
what one great soul will yet return to me
from conquering this sea's subtle force;
and who then mock our triumph with our failings?
For far more deeply fathomed will be our cause
and far less deceiving will we be, free
from all those loose and fickle reflections
that make us only what we seem to be.

Eden Farm

after the fall

Many a young traveller like yourselves
has trespassed through this cattle land and become
ensnared in that pasture, backed up
by the cattle against the high, wind-rubbed fence,
scared by their ebullience,
waiting for them to low their last and sleep,
since your first transgressors brought about
these present ways. They know the bull comes soon,
then they will let you go. They are fine
brown beasts, fantastic as fulgurite,
and will guard the gate, nuzzling the latch now
to test the security of their own internment.
They love to seek out things of flesh,
being themselves still fertile
and bearing the joyful burden
of their udders.
But they are a fickle host:
for the nature of beasts is first bestial
and then indifferent;
there is no empathy, for this world
is too obscure for them, I warn you.
You should take some time to understand the prurience here.
But if you strip down, know that the sun
is still roused and will play with you
with its smooth fingers before
digging in its nails.

Best to seek some shade, and let the trees
relate to you their ribald history
in the concupiscent splay of their limbs,
in their leafy veils and their shed rags of bark.
I know you have already felt
the ambivalence of this place:
when you came across the serried grass
of the garden, carrying your shoes,
I saw how the shards scored your bare feet,
for the grass can be sharp-bladed, slaughterous.
Not all in the garden is good.
See too the scratches on your arms –
the sanctity of roses is their scent,
and their profanity their unshackled thorns.
And when these beasts lie down in the field,
the grass softened by dew,
after the bull has been,
then you can leave quietly by the gate
back to your other life beyond
and to your own human terms,
past these scattered recumbents,
their bulk soothed down by the dusk,
their long, tired faces bearing
mouthfuls of insouciant cud.

The Difference of Distance

1

Talk to me of distance, of how to get there
from here, and I will tell you of another
and how I got here from there.
Here is a high moor of wildflower and low scrub
and twin tracks of Triassic sand channelled to
the headland's edge. We came up through dark fern
and timber, growth and undergrowth, a tangled enclave
out onto this exposed level of heath,
this harsh expanse anchored to hard basalt
formed stark in the dusk. We come here as if
for the first time, as if this place brings
its own time, our time its own place, causing
a halt in the transience, a pause to consider
what passes, its testament laid out in the track lines
scored across the moor to their inevitable stop.
As you go on, I wait, watching you go,
look out to the edge of land, enough to know
the limits of sight, like this place is its own discovery,
the lesson of journey, an atonement for my own
brief legitimacy, an intersection with self.
To think of going forward is to go
from now to a new reckoning, to track
the abstract of me there brought to fusion
with somewhere else and hard to make distinct –
to see myself in the thing, or see the thing itself.
Sometimes, where I am has enough validity.
So, as you go on, I pause in the stillness, in the muted light,
on the stretch of rutted sand, leaving the earth in lurch.

2

Already I have come far to get here, even in
the last few minutes, when each minute holds
to the last. I know how far it is to return,
to retrace with the eye the way back,
the marks made in the bleached sand grain
left to the run of wind and rain and salt;
to turn to what was by being stuck in what's here,
the stuff and matter of what got
raised up through heft and thrust
fathomed into the moment with me, that I can see
the heath's old face in its rough baize, the hard
bony look of its past, fraught, resolute,
all vanity lost in its coarse obduracy.
I want to see how it sees, to just stand
and be, brave to the vicissitudes of time
and only let go my reckoning at the full
measure of it. And still you go on,
becoming more separate, moving, passing,
unchecked, unpossessed, loosed from the earth,
heading to the edge as if only an end
can confirm the way. I look at you up ahead,
your body quick and intent, sure of its advance,
making the track your own path, despite
the hard ground, the long stretch of it,
the lateness. But here is my station;
here my forth and back, in the heave of my breathing,
the ears' dull pulse, the senses closed in;
here is the harbouring; here is my distance.

3

I look off towards the tilt and angle of the earth,
the income of night, at an egret locked
to an isthmus of rock in the ebb and flood of the wind,
before it lifts away, climbing into acres of height,
disappearing and reappearing, then arcing,
stilling, going back on itself, a sleek
insistent speck against the straightening sky.
This is what I see, and always see, intimations
of things lost and regained, retrieved and coveted,
held in a confluence of moment and memory,
like the bird circling in its current, turning
and returning, latched to its channels of air.

4

But here now comes a numbness, bunkered
on these tracks of dune. So much to go back over,
to sift through, to fix against, as I watch you
again pushing on, then turning to me, or to
a place left, or to yourself, beckoning
how it is good, as if I should guess how good,
that sometimes a hint is all we have to feel
the meaning in; that through you I should make
my choice, to follow or stay. Still you look back
as my thoughts weaken within the grip of dusk
sombre, vapid, losing themselves in me.
How far must you go from this spot
before I am only aware of myself, not you?

5

I want to tell you…I want to tell you
that I went on, that you didn't know it but I did,
that I cut from the track, onto the heath, across
the gorse's rough threshold, onto a clutch of new ground,
saw what has not been seen, brought back
the sense of discovery in my bone and flesh,
spoils of salt spray in the matted flumes of my hair,
sand blown into the nuances of my face, weeds
wreathed and draped around my neck and shoulders,
my body dripping with acts, baring the witness of my skin;
I want to tell you that I caught the headland's gaunt light
in my eye's lens, proof of my journey and my vision,
found vanquishment in the closing particles of light,
in the stillness that engulfs and consumes;
that I cry out to the bare gorse now and exalt.
I want to tell you, but I am still here, and you are already gone.

6

I can only tell you again how I got here,
dragging the past with me, hauling its body
onward, its gathered weight. But if there were one thing,
it would be my old man heaving out a stiff bench drawer
crammed and heavy with tobacco tins
chock with washers and bolts, nails and screws;
then another drawer, leaden with implements, saws, drills,
a boxed whetstone, oiled and readied,
a vice screwed hard to the bench edge,
strict particulars of life, gathered in
and stored, laden with use and purpose. I can only tell you
how I would watch him with them, never doing
anything with them myself except look at them,
things in themselves, to be got right in the head.
And if he wasn't looking, I'd touch them,
prize open the tins, the tins jammed in,
hard to get fingers to when you lifted one out,
like a piece of this heath stuck fast to its hold,
and stay, confined to the garage, the night
encroaching from the field and pressing in;
that escape could only be to bear, or to reckon on
or reflect; to watch out the light there, inert,
the sun palling behind the parading dusk
above a field line that still fixes and limits and forebodes.

7

This is where we are then, bound to our grounds
and to our ends, the facts and imaginings of our day,
whilst what stands apart from us, the raw heath
at our feet or the land's edge, what stays or beckons us,
importunes our decisions and our acts, holds us to the need
to home or to embark. Suddenly I am aware
of your body warm in the air next to me,
of your breathing, of the enclosed scrub at the track's halt
where I have come to be. I look at the place like it is
a formal sight, introduced to, engaged with
then given back to its own space, like you have already taken
familiarity with it, though I know you only want
to share, and that my place had been back there.
You turn to me, at my having finally followed.
I can tell you, I say, I can tell you why.
You look into me, like your eyes find my cause,
my long conditioning. You need to unlearn, you say.
You can be there or here, let everything be in its own place,
only you need move, then it will be different.
You look out again to the far spaces. I walk around
as if to see what you mean: to try to find
reparation now in the roots and covering of the heath;
appeasement in this flat, ancient plateau;
restitution in the sand lines stretching away,
staying their own course, narrowed and foreshortened
towards the edge of land and sky, ready to redeem.

Just hard to make distinct, myself in the thing
or the thing itself, the details crowded in
on the dusk, the light closed down, all distance gone.
If what you tell me is true, let us make the going back good,
knowing that the return can be new.

Stone Gatherer

In aubergine at the water's edge
Stone picking, bringing small, glassy
Stones back for the supper table;

Home to be washed, then dried
Over the stove, nearly good to eat.
Wild and dashed along the shoreline

You stooped to gather them, only
Those smooth and rounded, with the right
Solemnity of a peasant woman

Bent among abundant fields.
And when you returned unannounced with that
Surprise of pebbles, I hugged you.

Tomorrow's dinner will not taste
As nice as you did then, fresh from
The sea, and arms full of new crops.

The Skaters

Unfathomable, you stood stiffly like a wave
Before breaking. We had crossed the strand,
Breaching the old silence of the flats
Stretched out to the water margin
In the distance, and stopped to talk.

The sands, rippled and blistered, reminded me
Of great iced-up lakes further inland,
Or an old skating scene, and I whispered
In your ear der Neer's frozen vision.
'The cold,' I said, 'outlives them,'

As I thought of those simple figures, of barge casks
Heaved to the rough banks, the men
Huddled in their coats, the air
Dampening as the light failed,
And you, warming against me. You said,

'Once we would have rent the crisp ice,
Rushed across its surfaces,
Instead of this late vigilance of a coast.
But now we too freeze, harden like the past in us,
Or the world's, like a frosted root.'

And I understood that, your
Bold ambiguities, your need to reply;
That last season together, looking back
Upon our frozen lake of years.
Already we were wintering in our history
And remembering before the cold outlived us.

The Hover Fly

The hover fly hovers
outside my window,
the function of its wings
steadying it:
a haloed ring
around its crushable length.

Often in its beat I see
the single, faint didacticism
of its purpose,
definition beyond its worth,
wavering there,

elegiac on the air's light rhythms
sounding the hum of hundreds of wingbeats
on this difficult, still, uncomfortable heat.

Imprisoned in its brevity
its frail instinct hammers in its cells.

Thames Ditton Churchyard Revisited

Suddenly I am in the churchyard again,
Under the yew's great bruise of shade,
Treading worm mounds and new mown grass,
Low crows arcing towards some place of rest.
Then the wind comes up, gusts coursing
Out of nowhere like sheets of unseen ghosts.
Names rattle on the headstones; the gifts of words moan:
Monuments to quick life greyed out in the windy shadows.

It blows me back ten years ago
When I walked my lunchtimes here the same;
And nothing is altered – the church, the trees,
The neat scattering of tombs; all the unknown
In the one stasis of death.

I work back into my life, hunker down
Into old depths; tend what once I'd left;
Come back to a past riddance having followed
The course of sadness down to this familiar earth.
Only those above soil suffer still,
Making their ruin of time.

And yet I find within this dormant bane of ground
This churchyard's great untruth:
Its measure of my continuance and its right;
My course of life marked out still
By these same, dull, inveterate stones
Which stand consolingly inane;
A solace of retrieval
In the sad dearth of return; granted passage back
Along the tread-line of the grass path leading round
Amongst the sunk and leaning plots
Where none can now reflect or think ahead.

So I stare into the hard face of the wind,
Let the high sun flesh out the rounds of the day
And await the bony light of winter.

Leyton

Coming down for the last days left to us
this visit, time went quickly, streaming in
from the east where we were soon headed,
fast as reflection and as hard to make last.
We sat in the back room of my brother's
untended house, with its peeling walls
and nicotine-stained ceiling,
our bodies shivering in the cold
as the afternoon closed in early and dark.
Where do we go from here? I asked.
Back to the new country, you said, as the snow
fell upon the garden, covering the cannabis plants.

We sat before the small gas fire,
imbibing the soiled neglect of the place:
the dust on undisturbed surfaces;
sink grime and toilet stains –
a scale of dribbled piss about the rim –
imagining the germs breeding in all that cold
like formidable lovers on frosted sheets:
unlike us later that night, in a bed most slept in,
you cold as marble, and me dry as old coals
for the act, and still loath to provoke our leaving.

Nearing evening my brother walked me
to the butcher's shop and the supermarket
on the High Road, his black coat
white in the blizzard. I'll remember all this,
I said, trying even then to prevent
its passing, as we bore the sausages and the wine
back to the house, making each event
struggle against its instance,
hankering for it to last even as it died;
until it was he and I saying goodbye the next day
to more than ourselves, but to another glue of time
clinging us only to its passing,

better men than I have suffered here, grasping for wealth
in nothing but the poverty of moments
that become eventually just visions in the head,
changed into things even more yearned for.

Hart Field

When my old man called my name down the dark afternoon
I felt his voice to the core of my sudden shiver,
The sound echoing across the field from the far fence
Where he stood in his hooded, russet anorak,
A dim figure in the failing dusk, calling me in.
Sometimes a sound comes down centuries, becomes
Felt for more than it is: a bell toll or a raven's screech;
A hound's bark, a caterwaul, a veiled warning,
A tired animal calling for help amongst its own kind,
Each lasting all down the world's long age.
But of all sounds ever made came this one frail name
Unmingling itself out of the night air, baying
Through the cold from the edge of the distance, blasting me
To that arbitrary spot, bringing me suddenly into being.
I turned to face it, looking back to the fence,
Confronting the wind's raw razor's edge
Cutting my eyes to tears, my hands plunged
Into the pockets of my windcheater, singled out
Alone in the long grass of a timeless field,
The sound piercing the mute air, implicating me
Then gone, but all the darkness still listening to it.

Scrumping

How silently we did thieve and eat of that
apple cache, scrumped from the boughs
in that dark private arbour of over-laden trees;
spoils of unspoilt fruit spilt into hands
like rain from shaken branches; to take
of what the good flesh offered all we could
till sick with gourd. They were the reward
for our guilt scorned like the cores
stripped of skin and flesh and tossed to ground
and useless except as evidence
of plunder, till their sodden corpses
rot to mulch amongst the coming years.
But when we left there, others came,
honest foragers and scavengers,
to eat of those remains, feeding
on the sour brown pulp and pip like it were
more luscious fodder. They followed us back,
picking up other scraps from gutters and bins,
approaching meek but covert.
Their hungry eyes fixed us
and their twisted mouths asked
to have our cores whenever
we came there for our feast.
We looked at one another:
they would take our old bodies too, we thought
if we were not to be buried or burned.
But they know well the virtue of leftovers,
whose pillage bears no conscience;
they too understand that the secret
to fulfilment is never finishing.

The Bottom Fields

The time came for me to ache again
for the allotments and cemetery ground,
the overgrown track backing onto the houses,
old convolvulus, cow parsley, ragwort,
ravelled about hedges leading in slow descent

to a muddied stream along the osier bank.
It was as if such images
had hardened in the mind and become
brittle with age, like bone,
snapable into fragments,

as the scene showed itself in the glow of lamps
from the lanes, lighted through the dark day;
in the wind gusting through dusty sedge;
the mutter of leaves; the slow-footed,
gradual distancing from home.

Each morning we took that walk
down from the high ground into the bottom fields,
their shallow declivity finally reaching
the bog land, and the railway embankment
of russet gravel chips,

a route through it over wet clay and slop
beneath a black brick tunnel arch
to the farms, an echo of voices
splintering above us in the dark vault
of the immense roof.

Meek and salutary,
we acknowledged the rough disorder of the place,
coarse and unkempt after the streets
and the small gardens kept checked
from this mess beyond.

We kept our eyes fixed to ditches
and the dishevelment of grassways
worn to mulch and dead weed; the prospect
through the tunnel arch of silo stench, cattle dung,
the earthy, brown smell of pulled beer.

Women Digging Potatoes
after Van Gogh

Their hands finger the small rounds, like stones
Cloaked in earth, and dump them into piles.
They are large bodied women, bending in heavy skirts;
Silent commentators of ambitious days

That draw in across the open polder; working
In their slow, perfunctory progress and long task,
Their backsides pointing upwards at the windmills
Which forage also in an awkward element.

And what is the inelegance of the soil
But something they inherited with their birth;
An ungainly earth, its ugly, swollen ground;
As they gather up its knowledge in their hands.

These are the reclaimers. These are the peremptory
Processionals wielding these acres,
Stooped across the dirt, going by the rhythm
Of the soil. These are the travailers of fields.

And theirs are devotional movements: notice
The pious backs, the supplication in the bones.
The worldly course steers round their unprecocious craft.
Beneath these muddy features are angelic faces.

Couch Adrift

That painting you did of the old sofa
tilted slightly at an angle upon loose, strewn,
screwed up pages of old newspapers and girlie magazines –
Couch Adrift off a Lee Shore –
made me think of the vague lilt of humour,
the not quite upright seriousness
of good artistic method which spills over
from your life. Something more telling
always there to mock those who presume.
As when, peering at the rough water,
we notice the pink, naked nymphs
asplay in the crimps of the sea,
and point them out to unsuspecting
others come to look for more
littoral truth. I think this is the model
for the many ironies that lurk
unassumingly in life and art:
to show what is, through what might also be.

The couch leans to leeward
and the water nymphs play beside.

Be always before me, brother,
looking back knowingly from your kingdom of paint.

A Prospect of the Sea

for James and Natasha

What pales you now, O my daughter,
here at the beach's open edge
watching the wild boy take on the sea
and make mad war against the waves?
Let me teach you temper over awe,
control over innocence, faith
to the extent of peace, whilst I unknot
the fear from your tangled eyes.

The cool sea goads you, but the earth
draws you back. You point to the mass
of shrubs and trees up on the hill behind
the coast road like it is the strong pull
of the land you feel suddenly
drawing life again out of the eerie wet
towards the earth's warm soils and pulps and viands.

For you know the sea has power
to lure and betray, its white lips pouting
with ranks of serried swords for teeth.
How it smells fear, lives to feed its vast black belly
and once roused roams for more to imbibe
into its tough, sleek muscle. Then know too
that at dusk its skin is mercury,
molten to the base of the sky's grey curtain;
that by day it is some thick, green, chemical scale
covering deep, treasured bones;

that the body of the sea lurches
forth and back in its huge basins, thinking the earth
is merely grist and shale and weed;
that the sea has no mercy, even the sun
wasted on it, and all light lost.

I carry you, clung around my hip,
out of the water, though you have dipped in
no more than a toe. But we shall come
to it again and you will bear its ways,
face its complex forms, when you have learnt
to tame the abstracts in its blood.
Like he who rides out on it now
flat out on its back and head down in its jaws.
I let your body's shudder run through my own
as I tread the way to shore, the only man
who could have conceived you, and can see
you safe; coming back to your mother
becalmed on a towel that claims
a small spot of sand where the sun
is brightest and best spent.

Times Like These

in memoriam J.A.R

Times like these make me think
how what is past remains with us
though it is never understood again
like it was at its instance;
and the more remembered, becomes but
another remembrance of memory on memory
each one less certain and less clear.

When I knelt to remove your socks
because you couldn't reach your feet,
the age-wracked, awkward shell of your back
too unremediable and unyielding
beneath the papery skein of your flesh,
I felt all the pain of your sadness
ingrown in you like those long tough
yellowed nails; its smell turned as sour.
But, I thought, there is more to you than this,
than the slow penance done for being old.
Rather, a trust in life itself which justifies
the core of instinct still sustained
within the brittle husk – that form
which proves such certitude almost
an untruth, crushable in a hug.

In the end, ignoring the bone's ugly cracking,
resting your punished arm upon my arm,
let me hold again the intrinsic self
that I know and have always known,
but have left too often, and often
for too long; let this be with me more
than that last crooked image of you
outside the home, waving from the porch,
which hurts and denigrates,
where all is memory on memory, each one
nothing more than differently imposed.

For here is the irony of transience:
born with us and permanent from the start;
which sees us come and go and finally go,
and always presaging the end.
We bear our partings too deeply,
like that last leaving confounds again
the time we tried return ourselves,
together in our deepened sense of it
for being so reverent and so short.

But when we go from one another
what remains more is neither loss
nor hope nor valediction,
but the faith to recognise
the passing; that what has been
retains its own validity apart
even as the source of it weakens;
another caul kept in the needful regions
of the heart, by which to justify
our severance; to reconcile
my separateness to your own
and make my separateness whole.
We stay what we have been
each to each other, our lives resolved
more than all we recall.
What we have shared endures as one,
even though we redeem alone.

Transitions

That is my dead father standing up there
In his shorts beside the vegetable patch
His white legs thin as a gull's,
The puckered bulge of his knees
Pointing out towards the sadness
Of the plot. Most of his life
He worked this small corner of the garden
For its few crops, till too weak to tend them.
Around him now the ruined plantings:
The beans bowed over their frail stems;
The peas drooped across their string lines.
And somewhere in the centre,
Beneath a curved shield of stained plastic
Where only the grower knows what yields under,
The neglected pulps of some once potential fruit
About to fall to their bed after a tired year,
Their bitter bodies given up.

Watchful lingerer, feeling the last of the sun,
There to share the crop's demise
As if to mark the sudden point of passing,
Knowing the earth bears a while then takes in.
Grey eyed ruminant, goer into death,
Not knowing that the transition takes long,
Watching the slowness
Riddled everywhere through the earth;
Only the quick end lurking.

A Wiltshire Church Open Day

Soft sermons were what they gave me
In the belly of the church: cold mouthfuls
Of words to live by, like the old man in a frock coat,
Gathering my left hand like a hymn book
Releasing a nuance of hope in the meek form
Of a blessing to my unconvertible spirit:
'Thou shalt have a brief life but with
An eternal semblance.'
Whilst the choirboys offered tea like sacrifice
To us the preserved ones still,
Alone in our seeming longevity.
Behind the hymn board, an apse wall
Full of old artistry from the fitted scarlet carpet
To the high vault of ancient wood.
And in the windows a host of stories.
And the pale tombs enclosed the dead
Like flesh and bone about the hidden soul,
Marked with parables of carved brevity:
'As you are, so once was I;
As I am, so you will be.'
It is the names too which conceal
Memory, etched on transept floors.
Here whole histories hide,
In the mute, distended past.
And in the hush a million prayers.

Hard cheese and strong beer were what
They gave me in the bar of the pub,
Later, amongst talk of other things,
With the view across the wedged green
To the higher ground, and the church
Still preaching from its stone.

Losings

in memoriam J.E.R.

1 Drought

Your earth once boasted oceans, basins,
fulsome pools held perfect to the brim.
Now, from your pale ground, only thin spills
drip into parched, shallow, open hollows.

I shall bear you through this drought,
cleave closer to your dry beds until
the rains return to restore and fill you;
else founder too on your wasted silts and dust.

2 Cancer Ward

Draw the curtains round the bed,
Enclose them in their pain and dread.
Call all our sufferings heaven sent.

The earth shall bear what must be rent.
But which should be the prouder now:
The glistening scythe, the clodded plough?

3 Chemo

I go out into the garden, not to desert you,
but to tend the ground a while; to turn
the earth over into more manageable chunks;
to let my own agonies work themselves out
through the strong, tempered tines of the fork.

Nothing compares. We are too separate.
Inside, unable to unbear, you sit
with more pain than life should know,
staring down at a broken nail.

4 Ending

Oh that we should have such life
to hold each day as intimate, that nothing mar
the gains of love which distance so much strife;
that life should be so close, and death so far.

Oh that we should have such death,
so noble, so gracefully faced; to calmly guard
each moment sacrosanct, and bear each beat, each breath;
that life should be so simple, death so hard.

Festival

1 The Leaving

Back along the field line where this piece
of the earth's vast mass and form stretches on
between the uneven steeps of the valley,
through cold air rich with mist and dusk,
we walk together in slow departure;
out of a fray of pipes and strings and voices,
the music still sucking at our ears,
loosed seels of sound from the great tents,
muffled articulations breaking
cover and undergrowth and darkness.
Music as reveller, pleading to us
its cause. At our feet, the last heavy lie
of splayed light, leaden, stark, grafted hard
to the cordoned ground, to the matter
of the field, as the field's surface dampens,
borne off by the mist towards the floor
of the valley, beyond the music, the light,
into a grainy distance. I watch it darken away,
solitary, hesitant, unchecked,
as the night draws inevitably in,
and hardly notice the slow firm easing of your hand
into mine, the deft instinctive impulse
of palm pressed to palm, fingers to fingers,
cold flesh yielding to warm, as we walk connected
away from the festival's vital heart.

Unsure, ignorant or wrong, still I start
to question what it is I am again,
even this place and moment, the instance
of good that makes me always subject
to its loss; this quickening life; the sense
that each day must be reckoned against its end.
As if a hand cannot connect enough
to stay the lurch and fear of being;
to hold or falter alone, despite each other.
Even your whole body, composed, assured,
or bared, sleek, succumbed, drawing me in,
cannot fuse the immense interstices between.
Here it is the dark which divides, the cold
which separates, that this lock of hands,
the low, shared implacable drift of sound,
only implicate more the space in which we walk.
I look down, watching my feet move with yours,
the ground passing, letting the field bear us
against the sad vulnerability of skin.

If we tend it right the field will sustain, gift back.
It is of us, as of the earth, as much a part.
There are no laws, only rites and rituals
to understand this; how we have trudged
line and furrow; come at night with lanterns,
flaming torches, lighted the bones of wicker men,
made harvest bows to show to greying skies,
danced in hallowed circles round monoliths of stone:
offerings to whatever is to come.
As it is here: the low moon burning yellow
at the horizon; the plane trees plaited through the mist;
round the rings of tent posts fiddlers dancing:
bound with the field to the world's hard turning.
As I, our feet in equal rhythm, brace against
the on-come of time, holding to you, crossing
this patch of the earth like it is suddenly
an intersection of longing and dread,
marking what would remain of us,
the prospect of us here against the force of close
and parting. I was a braver seer once,
knew what it was to perceive the world
clear, precise, unfeared, shared with another;
anchored, confronting the uncertainty of years.

It could be so again, together on this ground,
gathering all my future into your hand,
wielded at the hip, that this moment seem
like my whole coming chronology
tamed upon this field's daunting spot, firming
my hand's subtle hold on yours, clutching your grip
thin but strong, high up to your wrist's delicate hilt.

2 The Repton Warrior

Only bone or stone or dust will prove
that we have been and done and died.
Where they found these bones, beneath a village churchyard,
smothered, subsumed, clinging to dirt,
the field had long harboured them.
Now they are brought up, brushed from the earth,
desoiled, arranged on a trestle close to their
last measure and shape, to their right form
that lived the air, hung their body's weight
before they fell. Beside them in the ground,
a sword, unclutched now, clogged with ironed age;
man and warrior, body and weapon,
caught at the instance of end.
Difficult to reconstruct from this
these bones' full testament, the sullied separations
missing hold, loose extracts apart from the whole,
the once body of time unowned except
by what can be hinted at or guessed.

Somewhere lie too the years left behind,
the hurtling forwards into absence and fight,
the lonely pursuit of purpose
where nothing inspires more than what has passed;
the ache of some less brutal human touch;
a whole heft of history come to be
on this field. But here only is memory's hollow,
the empty husk of enactments laid out now
like pieces of a bracelet missing their thread of being.
No thought, nor feeling, nor valediction
stays in these meagre marrowless tubes,
that what is left is only the shell, not the core,
become the bone's lasting untruth. Sometimes
the only recovery is that of loss.

3 The Bushdance

What I am is what I have been and will be,
the lone trajectory of myself, passing
along a narrow track against the valley's rise.
We are up on the hill slope, away from the main body
of tents, on the other side of the river's course
unseeable below; distracted from our leaving,
lured to the faint light of the hall's beckoning.
Inside, we merge into lines of dancers, join
a configuration of partners and positions,
bound in patterns of strict accordance,
and commence on the count of the music.
I hold to many hands, touched, gripped, slapped;
dance in rounds of four and eight, in rings
and baskets; tread, stomp, slide the ancient boards,
propelled by the clamour of instruments
filling the hall to the raftered roof. Somewhere
amongst the flock of folk you pass, forming
your own paths of intersect and angle.
I feel your hand again, held quickly and let go,
gathered in to me, honoured and then gone.
I look at the space now occupied by you
as once by me, the same space, but separated
by time. Then, moving forth and back in time,
both of us in the same time, separated by space.
As if this is our triumph and our tragedy,
to be now, and then, here, and there.

Breathless, we emerge, once more outside,
faces quenched in the cold occluded air,
and walk back across the river towards the fields.
Except where we return to now is not
a point of heading or departure, but of
singularity, realised out of what just ensued:
a knowledge of the boundaries in which we each play,
and by which we are validated,
amongst our dread and our desire.
Quickly I reach and gather back your hand,
letting mine in yours confide, with all
the vicissitudes that confine us apart.
For its touch is the measure of something greater
than what I fight, or anticipate, or fear;
it bears the fact of us, the marrow in the bones,
the nerves in the hollows, the sense and flesh
that limit and allow us be, fixed into this darkness,
to the moist ground of the field that turns with us,
as we walk back towards the tents,
our leaving. Here is the joy of it,
and the sadness: that we must know ourselves
alone so we can bring ourselves together;
our separateness that enables hold;
like the voice to the music, the dancer
to the dance, the field to the earth; as now,
for us, here still on this ground, in this place,
in this cold night, hand needing hand,
that what I am is what is, in this moment's lasting.

The Chickens at Summer Keep

Look at the strange, ugly perturbations
of these birds, and the short, absurd,
perambulating necks tapered
like their stuck-up arses
as they walk across the lawn.
I snatched the last day's eggs from the hutch,
neat and residential, then watched
as these three suburban chickens
raced towards my crude purpose
like disgruntled housewives, chasing
off a scrumper in their brown pinnies.

Kangaroo

The kangaroo lies reclined upon its side
like a Modigliani nude.

Upright, it squats knowingly
like a Buddha.

Dead beside the road it is
a mess of meat and fur;
someone knocked down
in a grey, tawdry coat.

When it moves quickly
there is the duff duff duff of it;
the intermittent landings
like a butcher's cleaver
hacking through meat and bone.
When it moves slowly
there remains in the L's of its legs
the sloth of some old geometry
come down to us in a stiff lollop
of confused meaning.

Its art is metaphor,
from the shuttle of lower jaw
to the jut of head and foreleg
out of the slit envelope of belly.
And between the brittle egg of the skull
and the boulder of the hip
is the soft impress
left by the warp of evolution
that once lay down there to rest
preparing for the platypus.

Pigeons

Once upon a time I would stand in the hallway
Of the old mansion block flat and watch
The pigeons that lived out on the window ledge
Of the light well, their grey waddling bodies
Feeding, crapping, mating, dying there,
The bones of their dead encrusted
On the same small narrow perch with the rest
Of their waste. I laughed off their existence
Without sympathy, secure in my own life
And so much possible still.
This morning I watched another pigeon
Underneath a railway arch at Surbiton station,
During my long, dull, daily commute towards death,
Its feathers plumped against the winter
As it walked along the crap-caked girder
Amongst the hard cream of its own filth.
And I sadly felt its cold, and understood,
Unable now to laugh it off.
What has changed in me is hope:
I don't trust to so much now,
But see only the hollow facts
Before any faith or redemption.
I sense a pigeon's life bearing in on me,
Like the pigeons on that window ledge –
Looking back at me more knowingly,
Prying stoics in deft proximity –
Watching even then my days revolve
Through feeding, crapping, mating, like their own.

Horror scope

The planetary alignment today suggests
my normally tranquil and imperturbable demeanour
will be upset by the influence of the moon in Pisces.
Now I don't know so much about the moon, or fish,
but I can say this: that if the facetious
gob-shite who prognosticates this stuff
doesn't get the hell out of my life every day
with his assumptions about my traits and destiny,
I'll write a very nasty poem about him
then go and muse upon the moon as it swims
serene and nonchalant amongst the indifferent stars.

The Inlet

The inlet laps and mouths to me.
It says: 'Bear me well,
For I am old, older than I look;
Bear me like I bear the rocks
Upon my shelf,
The weed at my side,
As old as I.'

The beach lies bent, narrow, tapered
Like a boomerang.
On the edge of the shoals
I walk through the loose debris of the shore
Listening to the sole-squelch of my boots
In the inlet's soft mulch,
Their shell-disturbing tread
Over the rocks,

As the salted, prawn-full depth
Raises up its stench
To the soft wind off the grey water,
The water surface full of cloud,
Its ebb and flow
Combing out thin fringes of weed
In small pools
Where lank tufts, soggy and stagnant,
Cling to the mottled scalps of the stones.

On the stiff tines of the bank-side scrub
A dribbling of dew
Where the palsied river mouth
Yawns out of insistent life.

And above the bald sandstone cliffs a shock
Of gulls, white-breasted, watchful,
Patient as thought,
Perched on a bare branch's overhang, before
The swathe again of wings through air.

Unseen, beneath the water,
Black-berried fronds
And the shells of incubuses,
The deep's archetypes
Washed in once from the greater sea
But bedded there now,
And which the ripples at my feet whisper of
With the tired breath of repeated knowledge.

The way it was
Before I came to this place
To bear its age
Making my path
Through its silences.
Only the days here are new.

Wood Gathering

Each night brings its own intimacies,
brief glimpses of things, like the motes
of dust floating up through the morphous
shafts of window-light that fall straight-hatched
across the room, in the blurred grain
of the evening before the lamps go on.
Here in the quiet spaces between actions
I hear the mute conspiracy of days,
the breath of their drear mouthings,
a clack of tongues in the confederate air,
their mime passing on into another dark.

Outside, amongst the trees, with the light
gone cold and grey and hard as pumice,
after all else has been done, I go through
the ritual of wood-gathering:
torch beam splayed across the dirt;
a long grovel for twigs plucked up
and snapped into manageable lengths,
bunched in the palm and clutched upright
like a shock of short stooks; my boot tracks
marking out a route across the paths
of rough sandy earth.
Then the beam swings away,
defines the line home towards the house steps,
brings back the gathering through the come of gloom.

Once lit, the sticks spatter in the midst
of the wood-fire's chamber;
sparks catch the split runnels of twig-bark
and trail into mellifluous flame
through the witch's cackle of the splintered log.

Settling, I try to feel congruent
to this consistent act that draws me through
the plot of each day's close, various
but with the same gnarled root of meaning.
How else to show conviction to whatever
is done, which life hangs from with a vulnerable hold,
which otherwise leaves cause to consider and dread.
How safe the routines that bind the frightful spill of time.
The stooped form meandering over coarse ground
unquestioning of the dusky earth; the strain
made welcome in the back's dull muscle;
the fire's vigil burning out the cold.

I let my body bear and winter out
the same strict enactments;
conformed to their passing, like the moulds
of pressed dirt left by a gum boot's tread.

Hawks Nest

Light years out from this thin cusp of beach,
beyond the sea's coruscated islands
and the clouds distilled at the horizon,
other worlds are spinning tales of their denizens,
but uncoloured, unpeopled,
and each as solitary as the other.

Look hard into the blue fenestration
that segregates us from them and you'll see
nothing but our own brandished light
until the penitent darkness allows.
But what dry rocks, what balled gases,
what sepulchered universes
clutter those spaces, include us in their scope,
unaware of our different heritage;
stars and worlds moving only for us,
distant points measured against our own
by which we mark our passing,
scale our purpose and our eternities.

This is why old men pause at the shore
to redeem some hope and sanctity from the waves,
seeing there the unerring repetition of days
seeming permanent; why you,
in the same bright realm of atmosphere,
shimmer in the sun's brief gift
without which nothing ever was,
venerable now and ambient on your face.
And if I'm lucky, or imaginative,
or uncynical, then I might see
your soul illumined also, as from a prism,
bearing no substance but its own many-coloured light
reaching out into its timeless place,
against which nothing not made blessed can be seen
except to prove the darknesses between:
things made only to exist and expire.

Memory

My memory is lazy.
Like the last time I peeked in on it
asleep in its dim-lit room
dreaming of itself.

Stone Country

1

There is no death or birth in this country, they say,
except as means to see the permanence:
the blackened trunks smouldering; new growth coming up;
the rock level's small instances of change. They say
that to understand this we will have to be
absent from everything else, out of our own time
and place, forget what brought us, and know it
by sense; come slowly to it, testing ourselves
over sand and boulders, alongside the hard-glazed green
of a river, bottoming the loom of a gorge to the mouth
of a plunge pool, the cold tongue of water readied
to carry us in, where you will swim out sleek,
easeful, hardly disturbing the surface;
on the slope of a boulder, the wet mark of where
you will sit after, its thin stain bleaching back
as you leave, like a trace of weeping
momentarily trying to recover loss. And so
it is. And still we move on. Only through change,
they say, will you know how things stay the same.

2

Then later, deep in the stone country, we are drawn
fully into this truth; amongst the outcrops of rock
steeped and angled against the earth's soft skin
and covering; looking out over the plain,
climbing up to goad out the view; the scale
of land low and flat across the wet; the distant
mass of plateau; the strong, sedentary calm.
And finally, returning down, moving into
the stones' hard form and structure, drawn
tentative into a sheltered enclave of jut
and cavity, under a jagged over-slab,
where a vast testament of art speaks out
from the great galleried face of the rock.

3

It is then, as you move away into your own space,
that the stone claims me, isolates, takes me in;
abstracts me from the run of time, here and now gone;
a quick pull of sense to some fixed, other presence.
Suddenly I am a dumbed, succumbed figure
amongst semblances, remnants; gloamed in their shade,
gleaning frail hints of leavings, ghostings; images
locked in the make and matter of the rock,
their coarse vernacular, howl and song of their unaging
like a glitch in the quiet of what has come and gone,
stretching back to the bared, discovered stone; myself
an initiate again, subsumed into their meaning,
reduced to a stare. Then there you are.
They are keys, you say, to how the earth is,
passed down to each in turn. What do you think?
I watch you come before them too as you
look for me to say something; find myself
re-grounded back from the rock, shucked off the hold
I had, standing where now I have to think again.

I peer harder up at the frail marks of art,
as if faltering between you and them, our world
and theirs, struggling to say, to express a sense
of this immensity, this measure beyond
what I know; too much for any moment
to hold; unable to anchor it to where I am,
and too aware again of you and I; of you,
as I am always aware of you, like it is you
showing all this to me, hard for me alone
to make words of it, to yield to my own sense,
delving into my thought, but become mute,
awkward, lost again in the course of things,
failing, unable to return a response.

4

Part of my story is this: a small boy sitting
in a time-distant kitchen, long fraught nulls
of silence taken fix of the air, the half-light,
fractured only by sounds other than speech:
plates, forks, knives, a family slowly eating,
breathing, looking; in the stress of quiet; sat apart
and unconnected, absented separately
as if into cold rock, its hard hold full of cause
and instance, but blank of any telling.

5

Then I am in your room teetering on the edge
of the bed, amongst the chairs, the desks, the books,
papers, clothes, waiting for the day to start,
the early light and shade angled through the slats
of the blind, sharp on every edge and plain of us.
Like we were, in that instant, small, discrete
particulars against the full of our lives,
caught in our own time and place, those tight confines
pressing in, demanding the necessity to brave
something of myself at last, some clear thought
for you to hold to, symbol or consequence
of being there with you, out of the vicissitudes
of the day, the contest of each new instance;
like I should always be interpreting the world
from the face of it, in the blunt thrust of its presence;
but my heart runs away hammering from too much
hold, unable to still enough, seeking flight and escape
and eked open, the pulse spilling silently onto the floor,
and foundering, like all our past slipping
between us; me struggling to save the moment
to realise and keep myself there with you
against the feeling of being already gone,
unable to find, grasp, articulate or redeem.

6

Is this then what led us to here? The sense
of what we had become; isolated, like bits
of stone broken from the whole; seeing the need
to hang on even through our unstrengthening;
seeking here to distract, or repel, or restore,
or find the permanence within the change;
to make stay our own stark markings?
I watch you walk off looking to leave
and move yourself on again; see the stone
hold ground to you as you retreat from it.
Still I try to offer something to you, sure,
instinctive, authentic, whilst the stone's own
thought and feeling calls out bold through its raw,
boned exposure, in the scores of line and groove
and plane, made clear and direct and exact.
Look here and you will know what to say.
But I won't know what to say, for nothing
has been passed down to me, except the need.
You stand apart now, holding your eyes
to a lens, focussed, composed – perhaps the lens
can explain the meaning more than the eye.
Even then I wonder if I can ever explain what I see
when all I see is you looking, becoming inert
to how we might continue, seeking what we've never had:
that I could ever give back to you equally of myself
so each self remains its own self, each life its own life,
amongst the roll of each day's light and dark.

7

I turn around towards the soft grass
and undergrowth stretching away behind,
clung to the harsh edge of this narrow spot
as you leave into it. I am a last look
beckoned back to the rock's remains,
as everything is always what remains;
the thin, skeletal, earthen pigments
handing down the irony of their meaning:
to make last what cannot last; holding up
to the mechanisms of the created world
their own stark image; while I stand,
in my dilemma of being, in the hard
immediacy of what it is to partake.
Maybe later, maybe later I will be able
to tell of it, gift it back; removed, distanced;
form it then from my lone re-fathoming
that doesn't involve you or me; outside
the urgency of what arises and expires.

8

They say that in this country all things return
something to each other, that all things sustain
all things: rock, tree, earth, animal, human;
eternal, ubiquitous. Like the yam, they say, yielding
to the digging, its ditch covered back
so new ones will always form the same.
Each change reconciled to its permanence.
I wanted to pull you to me, so at least this
could be offered, held, pressed in: that it could be
the same with us when we have left this country
and life again is our own time and place.

The Well

Someone brought the silence here, carried
its light body like sleep into this calm
charnelled spot, which, when you come here now,
can't be known, only its cold, stark exposure
felt as you arrive suddenly upon it. It is
a measure of depth and darkness, its innards
excrescent with dross and dank, mossed
and vined on the brick. Drop a stone
into the quiet and it will be subsumed,
kept and gone as if it never was,
like something never thought of, never done.

When I myself come this way, slow, tentative,
I see the well's form looming low, inscrutable,
out of the warm, soft ground, the same heavy soil
I tread. By day it harbours a piece of the blackness
that was there before any light; by night it is
subsumed to the dark, impossible to plumb
or fathom, or test. But you could try it; haul
the windlass round, draw the silence up
in the dry, empty bucket, look at it
and acknowledge; then lower it back
like an unwanted find, let it rest
at its unseen end and leave it
like you knew that was how it would be.

For me it is a sly, fearful silence resting there;
it pulls me down to it, wills me to hunker
and reside, like that which hangs between us
on the phone or across the room, a wait,
a yearn, a moment before and after breath,
a hole, an absence in what is thought
that nothing can resolve it, not even
the something said or not said, like it is
waiting for us to err, to falter, to fail,
to fall into it and be left in its lone place
till I am lost from you, your flesh, blood, bone
out of my feeling, unknown, devoid,
a quiet there beyond the realm of hearing.

If only I could harness it, get hold of it
somehow, I would set it apart from its depth,
lay out the rotten, sad hulk of it,
see it whole and separate, vulnerable,
let it lie and look at it, till it bake and shrivel
to its heart in the dry inane air around;
burn out its sound till it suffer and weep,
till it try to crawl back, a weak
ineffectual impulse to offer a small cry
from its core, some bleat, some tiny seep
that gives substance to it and sense
that we might touch it, like we touch flesh,
a cut in skin, that it bleed and hurt and know,
like I have felt your skin and bone and know.

Always though there is the null of it
that can't be brought out or got at,
which is the heart of it, turned on me,
its black face mocking so it is just
me and it alone, and I am anywhere,
in a closed room, an open field,
waiting on the phone, postulating
what can be done, what might be brought up
from what is held dumb within, each
looking to the other, wanting each to break
or resolve, like we can't move on till we change
or force or give; or until there, in its heart,
is the heart of me, is my own hard longing,
the far reach of feeling yet to be
articulated or interpreted;
like it is not the silence that I feel,
but my silence that I feel, as if nothing
of itself is; looking into the empty
light and dark, the inferences between,
searching in the mute hollows of air
for it to surrender its meaning;
but still waiting, the ground sinking in to me
at the edge of my footings, at the rise
of the well's void, ineluctable,
deep as the open heart. The only one
who brought this silence here was me.

Many a True Word…

Something always takes the eye and asks
something of it. Outside the Pan Pacific Hotel,
in the bleak morning monochrome of the plaza,
an old man rests up in his wheelchair
beside a concrete plinth in front of the carpark,
his body broad and squat with a great grey mane
of hair wired from his bald dome, handling stumps
of fruit into his mouth from a take-away container
on his lap, wearing the morning pathos in his face.
Against the open trunk of her car a mother
unloads groceries from a cart, her small child
dangling at the rear, turned forward forlornly.
Nearby, a man collects the trash liners,
perusing their innards, as a security guard,
saunters insecurely into the hotel lobby.
Hands pocketed, a boy walks by, music
insulating his ears, as a girl passes him
the other way watching her phone that it might
just grant her the meaning of it all.
A shop assistant rounds up the loose carts
and corals them back in front of the store,
talks to the man in the wheelchair who turns, gesticulates,
explains something to her: maybe his whole life
in a sentence, or just something he noticed.
I notice he has no feet, the too long bottoms
of his jeans rolled up to his ended shins.
He excoriates his nails into his head.
From the side he looks like Leonardo da Vinci.

Maybe I look too much in pity on these
innocent forms; brief lives passing through;
nothing to me except as what they seem.
But always the heart conjures off the eye
each thing in its lone significance.
Is what I see the image, then, or the reflection?
What is, or what I feel? My world, or theirs?
Another gorgeous Seattle day, the waiter says
gesturing the greyness, topping up my coffee.
Many a true word…

Early Morning, Ramsgate Harbour

The bunting flags of Union Jacks flap
ridiculously along the 18th-century balcony rail
of the Royal Harbour Hotel overlooking
Ramsgate harbour. Against their moorings
fishing vessels wait tethered like old dogs
for their owners to return, or closer in
stand awkward in the exposed dock, disarmed
and useless amongst their shadows.
In the distance you can just see the tide
pulling the vast mass of the sea towards
the vacuous blue of the sky, the sun
bleaching out the meet of sky and sea
and casting back a blinding swathe
of inane, indeterminate surface.
Every now and then a car passes,
and beside the red walling leading gently
down to the front, passers-by, their faces
blank in the flat light, promenade slowly, purposelessly,
as if facts and events are not quite happening yet
where all is lit low and hard and early.

So from my bed another day forms
out of the air, as such days would here;
shows itself new once more; meek, primitive,
disparate things yet to come into meaning,
connected only in place and moment
for the while I watch them, my last morning
here, already readying myself to leave,
hoping the day still has me certain in its hands
like again it might never let me go.

Canterbury Cathedral

In time there was enough seen to reap any more
from that cathedral's rooted might, or to be
interred longer under its stone, heavy with height,
confined to its law and precedent, the cold
set into it, the smell of its slow age ripe
in the moted light. Here were layers of past
gathered thick upon the surfaces, settled
onto walls and pillars and tombs, bearing
its mute significance, making it hard then
to disturb it or think it properly through,
needing time to understand and reflect.
So what were you yet gleaning, with your bold
immediacy, tending to the whole massiveness of it
in the dim intimacies of its space; giving yourself
to it, up close, so it might tell of itself to you,
like an old suffering or blessing, because
you would listen and not judge and know.

Finally we put out to the cloisters, into their
solace and release, beyond arch and opening,
onto the quadrangled edges, sunlit and shaded,
paths leading through the clustered beds of herbs
which drew you in till you were gone, succumbed
again to the catch of moment. Was it trite then
or innocent or irreverent to think
of monks here, silent and solitary, more than we
could be or suppose; to miss you even for
that instant, becoming ourselves separate,
isolated, like how it might be to be
cloistered long here, loitering with a god,
consumed within by what is unseen without.

Then there you were, sudden, confronting,
a brief harpy formed of heed and impulse,
shoving up a hand flat to my nose.
'I touched them all! Here, smell my fingers.'
Yarrow, wormwood, horehound, wood sage,
broom, dog rose, lemon balm, cowslip, hop,
straight from the care of flesh, the rush
of odours quick from the fingertips, hard
and abundant on you; the full of what
you do again breaking freely into the still
of the cloistered air, as if the years' slow
passings here conceded now at last to you
and allowed this hurry space; the fast, pent
unleash of feeling out of the brunt of things.
Oh, let me fear not nor censure the pace of either
place or time, that your presence be
the accumulation of my days now, apart
from any deep tradition bearing always back.

On the stone floor of the empty chapter house
you lay out flat on your back better to see
the high, ornate, spectacular ceiling, despite
the angled mirror placed conveniently
on the central wooden plinth. As I pulled you up
the span and heft of a thousand summoned years here
pulled on my gripped hands tangled in yours,
jumped with you into my arms, then fell away between to dust.

At Empress Falls

And so we come at last to this place, descending
into its cool darkness like we seek something out,
some lost part of ourselves dwelling amongst
these rocks and waters, old as the place is old,
but bearing something new. We come from
the familiar body of the surface, its scoured,
open flesh hardened and angled off, shaped
and reshaped, down to what is unknown, half
hidden, cowering beneath; as if to find sense
of things again, low in this underground,
a knowledge below what we know, unchanged,
anchored in the deep enclave of an arbitrary world
beside a course of water that finds its way
here too, staying the same by always passing through.

We have cause to be here, come from
our own separate places, beings who move
slowly now to discover out of something lost
that something else should start further into the end.
As if it takes coming here to know this, to bear ourselves
ready to accept, to abnegate ourselves,
away from the hanker, remorse, and regret,
as if that is all we are, things cast against
what we want to be and were, and stuck here
with our need to know the difference.
Down here the base constituent is dark,
with just enough light to create space between;
that this is what we have to navigate, fumbling
the thin glimpses, the measures in rock and time.

Sometimes all we have are vague things to cling to,
the faint idea of ourselves in the distances around,
an image fixed in the corner of the eye, moving with us
as dust moves, to be carried and to resettle
in another corner, seen differently, replaced,
revalidated, nothing ever wholly gone.
So we descend lower, in slow declension,
reach further into the stiff, intermittent dark
and light, following the water's course, stepping down
the face of the rock, sharp, high, sheer, dripping
wet from above, down through root and vine and niche,
as if to realise something more aware of us than us of it;
and going deeper, like it is always deeper,
like the only end is the continuance down.

At the bottom, we stand beside a small shallow
catchment at the base of the falls where the water
collects, stills, spills out. We look up, back, around,
away to where the water runs out. It is
difficult to see its course beyond rift and cleft
and impasse; when we have come through so much
already, to have ended up fragmentary, brittle,
the lost core of ourselves and nothing yet
to connect to, except the parts of our
sundered outcomes, trying to make some sense
of a whole body, and because we look from the same
point, and I understand your watching,
that we should become another part
of the randomness of this place, its abandonment,
its form and matter, the awkward, jointed boulders,
the numb worn edge and flank of the watercourse, the flat,
raw underbelly of the pooled, lifeless catchment.

And still we descend lower, following the water
across narrow folds of rock, down to its footings,
its slow seep along the baseline, where its run
funnels, levels and a brief planked crossing
bridges over, tight to the other bank.
Suddenly we are anchored there, steeped deep in cliff,
holding the bridge rail, pressed in to this
narrow, delved wedge of the cleft, the water
flowing under, all its height and fall and catch behind us,
and running away beneath us like so much time.

There are points where the memory always stops,
fixes on a mark, always gone, but always returning,
out of farthest backdrops where the past clings
and leeches an image back, around which
the immensity of everything else palls,
sucked down to a soft porous end.
I look into you as we stand separate apart, think
how we came upon each other, out of each
three year drift from the death of our lives,
open up to you all that has passed and ended in me,
around that point, born and relinquished, like I have been
yoked from a shell, loosed from myself, as I show you
the expanse of my time, the indistinct images
stretching ahead and back, as the memory scans,
catches; and then the sudden eagerness to fathom
the rest of life, its vague prospect redeemed into
possibilities by asking you here. As if to answer that,
I look ahead, up the long rift line wondering where
the path goes now, the water's course, questioning,
the scale of it, until you bring me back
to here, to stay here, to think only
of here, to hold to what is known, seen, felt,
like we hold the rail, cold, grey, strong between us.

It would be good to hold you too now, I think, to clutch
to you, nothing to hinder or harm except the threat
of the act itself, if I could be sure of that too
as of being here. Or is this only what I should expect
to find at such depth: the uncertainty of what
occurs after; to remain anxious, urgent, still to think
what else might come from what's already here.
What would I pull to me if I pulled myself to you?
You, or what I cling to in myself: the default of what
lies hunkered with me, both past and foreseen;
my surface world, stretching ahead and back,
always ahead and back, each start and end
of feeling, the distances which memory strives
to repeat and hope falters to renew,
as if I should draw the earth over me,
full of darks and hollows, unresolved matter
embedded in the heavy mass of years.
Or I could look with you at what is here now,
eking out of the earth and water; an unfamiliar instinct,
distinct to this place, emerging from the substance
of these steeps and edges, these ridges and fractures,
unlooked-for; the fact of us here, the smallest sense
wrought in the cauled fissures of the earth
like the water running into the rock holes, moulding
through the rock's separatenesses; that this
is a point I would reach to, or which the memory
would catch on; the knowledge that this is what
I must give pause to, that this is as far as we need descend.

We stand with what we have lost and might gain,
with all that is previous and next, goading us together,
like the water's massive fall which forced
us here; its run into the rocks beyond
like all that might be predicted and sought;
but to realise now that what we find here is not
the vastness of what forms our ground, before
and after, but each small indication of ourselves
wrought in the interstices, visible not as a whole
but in each part, not across, but by going down,
descending to confront it, discerned even
by the darknesses around, in enclaves of root
and frond and stem, the cool and the wet,
the sloughed emerald air, its old green smell,
the late dusk holding to the level of the ground,
signifying the moment still, and making it stay;
which holds me in its feeling, in a frail grain
of instance to reap from the immensity.

To know ourselves by the small particulars,
that carry the meaning, that fix and implicate us,
define, and show us to be, which never
can be changed or resolved, only taken in
and acceded, kept in their own place by others
we would validate them by, which include
and hold, for us being now deeper; to see
by these new intricacies, picked out within
the thin glare: the low shade upon your face;
the slow, deep, green dilation of your eye
glinting in the faint resolute hints of light;
here, now, stilled, not looking back or ahead,
where there is no hanker, remorse, or regret;
that this is what we are, that we have to descend
so far to see it, to where only we can go;
knowing that we shall leave different, together,
bound by all these new intimacies, the faint sound
of the water beneath, the planks easing to our crossing,
the air inert and clear; a meek insubstantial sense
that if this had never happened, nothing of us
would ever have been; as the water moves on,
feeling out the bed stones of its journey,
its relentless, sure, inevitable course.

www.ingramcontent.com/pod-product-compliance
Lightning Source LLC
Chambersburg PA
CBHW070942080526
44589CB00013B/1617